PARROTS

by Ruth Bjorklund

Children's Press®

An Imprint of Scholastic Inc.
New York   Toronto   London   Auckland   Sydney
Mexico City   New Delhi   Hong Kong
Danbury, Connecticut

Content Consultant
Dr. Stephen S. Ditchkoff
Professor of Wildlife Sciences
Auburn University
Auburn, Alabama

Photographs © 2013: age fotostock: 27 (ARCO/Henry, P), 1, 2
foreground, 3 foreground, 19, 46 (Berndt Fischer), 8 (FLPA/Neil
Bowman), 16 (Laurent Guerinaud); Bob Italiano: 44 foreground,
45 foreground; Dreamstime: 2 background, 3 background, 44
background, 45 background (David Dominguez), 5 bottom, 36
(Digitalpress); iStockphoto: 4, 5 background, 40 (Anand Sharma),
32 (Mayumi Terao), cover (Sergey Ivanov); Media Bakery/Tim
Laman: 5 top, 11; National Geographic Stock/Frans Lanting: 12;
Shutterstock, Inc.: 7 (C. Haessler), 20 (guentermanaus), 15 (Jianhao
Guan); Superstock, Inc.: 23, 24 (age fotostock), 39 (Minden Pictures),
28 (Photononstop); The Image Works: 35 (Rajesh Chakrabarti/
DrikNEWS/Majority World), 31 (TopFoto).

Library of Congress Cataloging-in-Publication Data
Bjorklund, Ruth.
  Parrots/by Ruth Bjorklund.
      p. cm.—(Nature's children)
  Includes bibliographical references and index.
  ISBN-13: 978-0-531-26836-0 (lib. bdg.)
  ISBN-13: 978-0-531-25481-3 (pbk.)
1. Parrots—Juvenile literature. I. Title.
  QL696.P7B57 2013
  598.7'1—dc23   2012000643

All rights reserved. Published in 2013 by Children's Press, an imprint
of Scholastic Inc.
Printed in China 62
SCHOLASTIC, CHILDREN'S PRESS, and associated logos are
trademarks and/or registered trademarks of Scholastic Inc.

1 2 3 4 5 6 7 8 9 10 R 22 21 20 19 18 17 16 15 14 13

Parrots

Class	Aves
Order	Psittaciformes
Families	Psittacidae (most parrots), Cacatuidae (cockatoos and cockatiels), Strigopidae (four parrots native to New Zealand)
Genus	Around 88 genera
Species	Around 386 species
World distribution	Nearly all species of parrots live in the Southern Hemisphere; a few species live in Mexico and the Caribbean islands
Habitats	Mostly subtropical and tropical woodlands; some species are also found in rain forests, grasslands, deserts, and mountains
Distinctive physical characteristics	Adult parrots are covered in a thin layer of colorful feathers; they have large heads, short necks, hooked bills, stocky bodies, and short legs; two toes point forward and two point backward
Habits	Very social; very noisy; mostly live in groups of the same species
Diet	Fruit, nuts, seeds, berries, pollen, nectar, and flower buds; some species eat insects; the kea sometimes eats carrion

Contents

CHAPTER 1
6 Colorful Creatures

CHAPTER 2
14 Clever Birds

CHAPTER 3
22 Life in the Treetops

CHAPTER 4
29 Natural History

CHAPTER 5
33 Flying into Tomorrow

42 Words to Know
44 Habitat Map
46 Find Out More
47 Index
48 About the Author

Colorful Creatures

With their colorful feathers and noisy songs, parrots have long captured the attention of people around the world. From the tiny yellow-capped pygmy parrot to the majestic hyacinth macaw, these amazing birds range in size from under 4 inches (10 centimeters) to 40 inches (102 cm) in length. The tiniest parrots can weigh less than half an ounce (14 grams). The heaviest parrots weigh more than 8 pounds (3.6 kg).

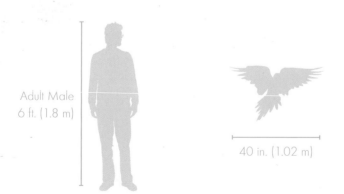

Adult Male
6 ft. (1.8 m)

40 in. (1.02 m)

Macaws are well known for their beautiful feathers.

Crown to Tail

Parrot **species** have a wide range of shapes and sizes, but they share some common traits. All parrots are plump birds with short, sturdy legs and four scaly toes on each foot. They have short necks and large heads. They also have powerful, hooked bills and strong, flexible tongues.

A few parrots, such as the pink cockatoo and the red-fan parrot, have colorful feathers on their heads that can be raised or lowered. Some parrots, such as the rainbow lorikeet and the scarlet macaw, have long tails that narrow to a point. Other parrots, such as the palm cockatoo and the blue-rumped parrot, have short, round tails.

FUN FACT! There are more than 380 different species of parrots.

Pink cockatoos can choose when to show off their brightly colored head feathers.

Parrot Plumage

A parrot's plumage is dazzling. Bright green is the most common color of parrot feathers, but many species have feathers in a wide range of color combinations. Unlike most other birds, male and female parrots of the same species are usually the same color. One exception is the eclectus parrot. The male is mostly green with a touch of red under the wings and a few blue feathers in the tail. The female is a brilliant red with a bright blue band around her neck.

Once a year, parrots shed a few feathers at a time and replace them with new ones. This is called molting. They molt an equal number of feathers on each side of their body so they can fly in balance. Parrots clean their feathers by using their beaks to pluck away dirt and parasites. This is called preening.

Male and female eclectus parrots are different colors.

Home Sweet Home

Parrots live in mostly tropical and subtropical **habitats**. These habitats range from rain forests to deserts and from lowlands to mountains. Parrots can be found in South and Central America, Mexico, Africa, southern Asia, Australia, and New Zealand. Only one species, the Carolina parakeet, was native to the United States. It is now **extinct**.

Most parrots do not **migrate**. There is generally enough food for them to stay in the same habitat year-round. But some parrots, such as budgerigars and cockatiels, live in dry areas. When their food supply begins to disappear, they travel to wetter areas where food is more plentiful. Some island-dwelling parrots also fly short distances to other islands or the nearby mainland.

FUN FACT! Large parrots such as African grays and macaws can live for more than 100 years.

Many parrot species are found in the rain forests of South America.

CHAPTER 2

Clever Birds

Parrots are among the most intelligent animals on Earth. Some parrots are even known to use tools such as rocks and sticks to gather food or attract mates. For example, the palm cockatoo beats sticks against a hollow tree to get the attention of nearby females.

Parrots can mimic many sounds. Some can even imitate human speech. Dr. Irene Pepperberg taught her African gray parrot Alex more than 100 words. Alex was not just a mimic. He could count and identify colors, shapes, and sizes. He could also communicate with Dr. Pepperberg by saying things such as "I want a nut" or "Come here."

Parrots are fast learners. Parents teach their young important survival skills, such as what to eat and where to find food. Young parrots also learn by playing with each other. They have mock battles and take off on wild flights. These games give them skills they will need to escape from predators.

Young parrots are very playful.

Incredible Eaters

With its bill, a parrot can crush open nutshells and crack the tough husks around seeds. Large macaws and cockatoos can split nuts the size of golf balls. Parrots also use their bills to build nests. They do this by either chipping holes in trees or digging holes in the ground.

Some parrots have brushlike tips on their tongues to suck nectar and pollen from flowers and grasses. Pygmy parrots use their tongues to spear insects out of tree bark.

Many bird species hold food with their claws and bend downward to eat. Parrots, however, use their claws like hands and lift food up to their mouths.

FUN FACT! Some parrots, such as macaws, must chew on wood to keep their beaks clean and sharp.

Parrots use their claws to bring food to their mouths, much like humans use forks or spoons.

On the Move

Parrots move around in many ways. They are strong climbers. Many parrots swing and hop from branch to branch or vine to vine. Parrots use their strong claws to tightly grasp tree branches. Some, such as the blue-crowned hanging parrot, even perch upside down.

Many parrots fly near the ground. They often fly in jerky, irregular patterns to confuse predators. When they are ready to perch, they fly sharply upward. Some parrots fly long distances above the canopy. Others, such as the night parrot and the kakapo, are nearly flightless. This makes it harder for them to avoid predators. They stay safe by hunting for food at night while most of their predators are sleeping.

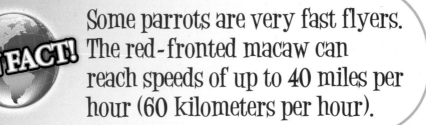

FUN FACT! Some parrots are very fast flyers. The red-fronted macaw can reach speeds of up to 40 miles per hour (60 kilometers per hour).

Parrots appear much larger when they spread their wings to fly.

Out of Sight

Many parrots use camouflage to help them stay safe from predators. Green feathers help them blend in with the forest leaves so predators cannot see them. In tropical forests, parrots are often the same colors as the flowers that grow in their habitat. Parrots that live in drier regions tend to be paler in color. This helps them blend in with their sandy, rocky habitats.

Some parrots stay safe by hiding from their predators. Ground parrots quietly take cover in tall grasses. Cockatiels lie lengthwise along large tree branches. In dry habitats, all of the animals share just a few watering holes. Parrots in these habitats hide from the other animals by drinking from the watering holes only at night.

 **FUN FACT!** Parrot predators include birds of prey as well as ground animals such as foxes and cats.

Some parrots are very good at blending in with their surroundings.

CHAPTER 3

Life in the Treetops

Parrots usually share their habitats with a wide range of other plant and animal species. This means that they have plenty of different foods to eat. Their diets are made up mainly of fruit, berries, seeds, nuts, flower buds, pollen, and nectar. Some parrots, such as the double-eyed fig parrot, eat grubs and insects. The kea of New Zealand will also eat carrion.

Many parrots live near rivers and streams. Sometimes water levels drop, uncovering clay in the bottoms of the riverbeds or along the banks of the river. When this happens, parrots flock by the hundreds to lick at the clay. Scientists say the clay provides parrots with minerals they need to stay healthy.

Large groups of macaws gather to lick at exposed clay.

Social Life

Parrots are very social birds. They often live in large flocks of the same species. Most species commonly form flocks of 20 to 30 parrots. Flocks can be much larger, though, sometimes even numbering in the thousands. Parrots **roost** together in trees and fly back and forth from their feeding grounds together. Many fruit-eating parrots **forage** in groups.

Parrots are noisy. They sing and squawk to attract mates or show distress. Their sounds range from quiet whistles to earsplitting screams and screeches. These sounds can often be heard from miles away. Young parrots make noise to beg for food. Parrots chatter loudly in the morning, evening, and when flying to and from their feeding grounds. Parrots are usually only quiet when eating and roosting.

Parrots work together to find places where food is plentiful.

Proud Parrot Parents

Parrots form pair bonds. This means that both parents tend their young together. Some parrots, such as lovebirds, mate for life.

Different parrot species mate at different times of the year. Most make nests in tree holes or rock cliffs. Some parrots use nests abandoned by other animals, such as termite mounds. A few make nests with sticks.

After mating, a female parrot lays between one and eight eggs in a group called a clutch. Then she sits on the eggs for 17 to 35 days before they hatch. The male brings her food while she incubates the eggs.

Parrot chicks are pink and featherless. Their parents provide them with food. They usually have enough feathers to fly by the time they are 20 to 70 days old. After the chicks have learned to fly, their parents continue to feed them until they can protect themselves and find food on their own.

Newborn parrot chicks look very different from adults.

CHAPTER 4

Natural History

Scientists are not certain how long parrots have existed on Earth. Scientists usually rely on **fossils** to learn the history of animal species. However, parrot fossils are fragile and easily destroyed. This makes them very rare.

In the Southern Hemisphere, where parrots live today, scientists have found parrot fossils that are about 15 million years old. But in 2008, a team of scientists discovered a parrot fossil in Denmark that dates back 55 million years. This makes it almost as old as some dinosaur fossils. Scientists were surprised to learn that the earliest parrots may have once lived in northern Europe. Some say that Europe's climate may have been much warmer at the time and that after the area began to cool, parrots traveled to warmer regions.

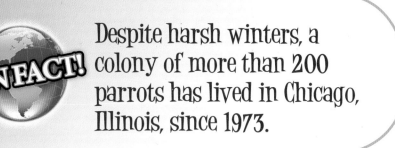

FUN FACT! Despite harsh winters, a colony of more than 200 parrots has lived in Chicago, Illinois, since 1973.

Fossils and skeletons help scientists learn about ancient parrots.

A History with Humans

Parrots have fascinated humans for thousands of years. Ancient Egyptian hieroglyphics show that royal families kept parrots as pets. In the 4th century BCE, the Greek philosopher Aristotle described what is now known as a parrot. He called it Psittacae, which led to its current scientific name.

In 327 BCE, Alexander the Great brought parrots from India to Europe. In the late 15th century CE, explorer Christopher Columbus brought parrots from Cuba back to Queen Isabella of Spain. Other European explorers and traders captured Amazons and macaws from South and Central America. Some parrots went to zoos, but most were captured to meet the demand for pets.

FUN FACT! About 17,000 parrots are brought into the United States each year to be sold as pets.

Parrots have been popular pets for hundreds of years.

31

CHAPTER 5

Flying into Tomorrow

Parrots are the most **threatened** of all bird groups. Almost one-third of the world's parrot species are threatened or **endangered**. This means that they are close to becoming extinct. Some parrot species die out because of natural causes, but human activities are a much more common reason for the disappearance of parrot species.

Habitat loss affects parrots' ability to survive. Some habitat destruction is because of natural disasters, such as hurricanes or drought. Other parrot habitats are ruined by a loss of food sources or the spread of diseases or parasites. But most habitat loss is a result of farming, logging, and the growth of cities and towns.

Logging is a major cause of habitat loss for rain forest animals.

Parrot Problems

Farmers often see wild parrots as pests. Parrots that live in the forests near farmlands frequently invade fields to steal fruit, vegetables, and grains. Farmers respond by shooting or poisoning them.

Each year, millions of acres of rain forest trees are cut down to make lumber and paper products. This destroys parrots' nests and food sources. As a result, many parrot species living in rain forests are at risk of extinction.

There are usually laws banning the capture and sale of parrots. But **poachers** continue to sell endangered birds illegally. They encourage poor people in villages to trap parrots. The villagers make money selling the birds to traders. Then traders sell the parrots to wealthy collectors for hundreds or even thousands of dollars.

Parrots fly into farms in large groups to eat crops.

Disappearing Habitats

Parrot habitats are also affected by human population growth. As cities and towns expand to hold more people, they take over parrot habitats. Parrots suffer from the loss of food and shelter. Most parrots do not adapt well to living near humans. However, some manage to succeed in their new environments. One year, a flock of wild parrots mysteriously appeared in San Francisco. They lived in the city's treetops and survived by eating food left out for them. Later, the parrots learned to forage on their own.

Many people around the world are concerned about shrinking parrot populations and are trying to prevent their decline. In regions such as Mexico and South America, people have created remote ecotourism resorts. Tourists can visit the parrot habitats and enjoy bird-watching. The local villagers make money selling goods and services to the tourists. The habitats are preserved, and the parrots are given a chance to thrive.

Some zoos allow visitors to interact with parrots.

Saving the Kakapo

The New Zealand kakapo is unique. Its face is round like an owl's, it has whiskers like a cat, and it can bark like a dog. It is the heaviest parrot species, and it cannot fly. Its feathers are thick and soft, and smell sweet like honey.

The kakapo thrived in New Zealand for millions of years. But humans arrived in its habitat 700 years ago, bringing animals and livestock. Suddenly, the kakapo had many predators.

By the 1950s, the kakapo was thought to be extinct. But in 1977, 18 male kakapo were found deep in the forest. The New Zealand wildlife service later found 200 more kakapo, including a few females, on a nearby island. The island was overrun with dangerous feral cats, so the wildlife service airlifted the kakapo in helicopters to safe, predator-free islands. These actions saved the world's rarest parrots from extinction.

The New Zealand kakapo came very close to extinction.

Conservation and the Future

Around the world, people are working to save parrots and their habitats. In 1992, the United States passed the Wild Bird Conservation Act making it illegal to import wild parrots into the country. All parrots sold as pets in the United States must be bred in captivity. Captive breeding satisfies people's desire for pet parrots and reduces poaching.

Zoos are also very important in saving endangered parrots from becoming extinct. The Spix's macaw of Brazil is thought to be extinct in the wild. Several zoos have breeding programs in hopes of one day returning the Spix's macaw to the wild.

Parrots face many dangers. By conserving their habitats and being aware of illegal poaching, people can help these magnificent and intelligent birds survive long into the future.

With our help, parrots will be able to fly freely in their natural habitats for years to come.

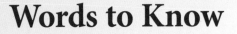

Words to Know

camouflage (KAM-o-flaj) — coloring or body shape that allows an animal to blend in with its surroundings

canopy (KAN-uh-pee) — the upper level of a rain forest, consisting mostly of branches, vines, and leaves

captivity (kap-TIV-i-tee) — the condition of being held or trapped by people

carrion (KAR-ee-uhn) — dead animal flesh

chicks (CHIKS) — very young birds

clutch (KLUHCH) — a nest of eggs

conservation (kon-sur-VAY-shuhn) — the act of protecting an environment and the living things in it

endangered (en-DAYN-jurd) — at risk of becoming extinct, usually because of human activity

extinct (ik-STINGKT) — no longer found alive

forage (FOR-ij) — search for food

fossils (FOSS-uhlz) — the hardened remains of prehistoric plants and animals

habitats (HAB-uh-tats) — the places where an animal or a plant is usually found

incubates (ING-kyuh-bates) — keeps eggs warm before they hatch

mates (MAYTS) — animals that join together to reproduce

migrate (MY-grayt) — to move from one area to another

mimic (MIM-ik) — to imitate a voice, sound, appearance, or behavior

parasites (PAR-uh-sites) — animals or plants that live on or inside another animal
or plant

perch (PURCH) — to sit or stand on the edge of something, often high up

plumage (PLOO-mij) — a bird's feathers, considered all together

poachers (POH-churz) — people who hunt or fish illegally

predators (PREH-duh-turz) — animals that live by hunting other animals for food

preening (PREEN-ing) — the act of cleaning and arranging feathers with the bill

roost (ROOST) — settle somewhere to rest or sleep

species (SPEE-sheez) — one of the groups into which animals
and plants of the same genus are divided

threatened (THRET-uhnd) — at risk of becoming endangered

NORTH AMERICA

PACIFIC

OCEAN

ATLANTIC

SOUTH AMERICA

Parrot Range

Find Out More

Books

Gallagher, Debbie. *Parrots*. New York: Marshall Cavendish Benchmark, 2010.

Hanel, Rachael. *Parrots*. Mankato, MN: Creative Education, 2009.

Haney, Johannah. *Parrots*. Tarrytown, NY: Marshall Cavendish Benchmark, 2009.

Montgomery, Sy. *Kakapo Rescue: Saving the World's Strangest Parrot*. Boston: Houghton Mifflin, 2010.

Owen, Ruth. *Parrots*. New York: Windmill Books, 2012.

Rockwood, Leigh. *Parrots Are Smart!* New York: PowerKids Press, 2010.

Visit this Scholastic Web site for more information on parrots:
www.factsfornow.scholastic.com
Enter the keyword **Parrots**

Index

African gray parrots, 13, 14

bills, 9, 10, 17
blue-rumped parrots, 9
budgerigars, 13

camouflage, *20*, 21
captive breeding, 41
Carolina parakeets, 13
chicks, 26, *27*
claws, *16*, 17, 18
clay, 22, *23*
climbing, 18
clutches, 26
cockatiels, 13, 21
cockatoos, *8*, 9, 14, 17
colors, *7*, *8*, 9, 10, *11*, 21
communication, 14, 25, 38
conservation, *40*, 41

double-eyed fig parrots, 22

eclectus parrots, 10, *11*
ecotourism, 37
eggs, 26
endangered species, 33, 34, 38, *39*, 41
extinction, 13, 33, 34, 38, 41

farming, 33, 34, *35*
feathers, *7*, *8*, 9, 10, 21, 26, 38
females, 10, *11*, 14, 26, 38

flocks, 22, *24*, 25, 37
flying, 10, 13, 18, *19*, 25, 26, *35*, 38, *40*
food, 13, 14, *16*, 17, 18, 22, *24*, 25, 26,
    33, 34, *35*, 37
fossils, *28*, 29

habitats, *12*, 13, 21, 22, *32*, 33, 34, 37,
    38, *40*, 41
history, 29, 30
humans, 14, 30, 33, 34, *36*, 37, 38, 41

intelligence, 14

kakapos, 18, 38, *39*
keas, 22

laws, 34, 41
legs, 9
lengths, 6
life span, 13
logging, *32*, 33
lovebirds, 26

macaws, 6, 9, 13, 17, *23*, 30, 41
males, 10, *11*, 26, 38
mating, 14, 25, 26, 41
migration, 13
molting, 10

nests, 17, 26, 34
New Zealand kakapos, 18, 38, *39*

(Index continued)

night parrots, 18

pair bonds, 26
palm cockatoos, 9, 14
Pepperberg, Irene, 14
pets, 30, *31*, 41
pink cockatoos, *8*, 9
playing, 14, *15*
poaching, 34, 41
predators, 14, 18, 21, 38
preening, 10
prehistoric parrots, *28*, 29
pygmy parrots, 6, 17

red-fan parrots, 9
roosting, 25

sizes, 6, *6*, 9, *19*
species, 9, 10, 22, 25, 26, 29, 33, 34
Spix's macaws, 41

tails, 9, 10
threatened species, 33, 34
toes, 9
tongues, 9, 17

weight, 6

zoos, 30, 41

About the Author

Ruth Bjorklund lives on Bainbridge Island in Washington State. She graduated with a master's degree in library and information science from the University of Washington in Seattle. She has written numerous books for young people, many of them about science and animals. An avid local bird-watcher, she hopes that one day in her travels she will see parrots in the wild.